A Beatty wooden tub electric washing machine with power-operated wringer, about 1916.

EARLY ELECTRICAL APPLIANCES

Bob Gordon

Shire Publications Ltd

CONTENTS

Published in 2010 by Shire Publications Ltd, Midland House, West Way, Botley, Oxford OX2 0PH, UK. Copyright © 1984 by Bob Gordon. First published 1984; reprinted 1998 and 2010. Shire Library 124. ISBN 978 0 85263 694 7.

Printed in China through Worldprint Ltd.

ACKNOWLEDGEMENTS
  The author is grateful to Marion Binks, Anthony Byers and Richard Hancock for reading and commenting on the manuscript; to Thelma Sayers and John Norris for their helpful co-operation; to David Coombs, editor of *Antique Collector*, for permission to use information from an article by the author published in the magazine in March 1982; and to Peter Mole for photographic work. The small photographs on the front cover are reproduced by kind permission of the Southern Electric Museum and are the copyright of Southern Electric plc. Other photographs and illustrations are acknowledged as follows: *Centenary of Service*, pages 5, 12 (right), 17, 20 (top), 22 (bottom right), 23 (top left); *Electrical Review*, pages 8 (top right), 11 (top left), 22 (top), 23 (top right), 30 (top right); Electricity Council, pages 11 (top right), 23 (bottom); *Electricity for Everybody*, cover; Goblin (BVC) Ltd, pages 20 (bottom right), 32; *Watford Magazine*, pages 3, 8 (top left), 24 (left), 30 (bottom), 31. All other illustrations were reproduced by kind permission of the Milne Museum, Tonbridge.

COVER: *Main picture: An Edwardian all-electric kitchen in which eight electrical appliances are installed, together with an electrically driven knife cleaner in the scullery; about 1908. Insets (from left): 'Paquet Special' iron made by Compagnie Paquet, c.1922; kettle, model 2642, manufactured by Premier, c.1926; fan by Metropolitan-Vickers, c.1936; water jug by Prometheus, c.1930.*

BELOW: *The electricity supply industry began at Godalming in Surrey on 26th September 1881. This sketch appeared in the 'Graphic' the same year and depicts the first power station in the world to provide a public supply of electricity.*

INTRODUCTION

Today we live in an age when electricity is taken so much for granted that it is difficult to imagine a time when electrical aids for the home were not available. Electrical appliances are, however, a comparatively recent innovation which followed the provision of public supplies of electricity, the first of these being switched on in Godalming, Surrey, on 26th September 1881.

At first electricity was used only for lighting, but as lighting gave off heat as well an obvious additional use for electrical energy was for heating. One of the first electrical appliances to be developed was the electric radiator, and by 1894 a surprisingly wide selection of other electrical aids was being manufactured.

Since that time a fascinating collection of electrical appliances has become available to the home, some to lighten one's labours, some to improve health and beauty and others to entertain and improve family lifestyle. Many examples of these appliances are described in this book: some are quaint, some bizarre, but all are of interest, especially to students and collectors.

It is hoped that readers whose interest in the subject is aroused by this book will seek more information by visiting one or more of the museums listed at the end of the book.

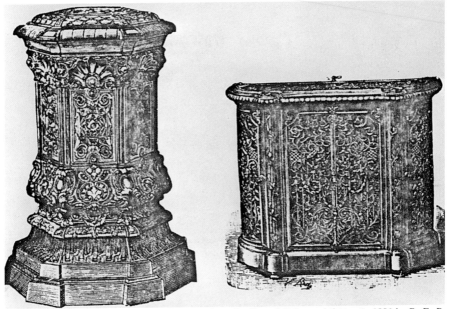

Domestic radiators were first exhibited in Britain at the Crystal Palace exhibition in 1891 by R. E. B. Crompton and H. J. Dowsing. They took a long time to heat up and gave no visual indication of heat.

HEATING AND REFRIGERATION

HEATING

In the latter part of the nineteenth century a revolutionary form of electrical energy became available which provided heat without the need for on site chemical combustion.

The first electric heaters were devices for converting electricity into heat. The way they worked was simple. A switch allowed electricity to flow through spirals of *resistance wire* called heating elements. These resisted the passage of electricity and the energy expended in overcoming their resistance made them hot.

Enterprising engineers soon set about inventing novel heating devices and by 1912 electricity was listed as being in use for 160 different applications. Heating appliances ranged from ornate cast iron radiators, with heating wires embedded in enamel, to cigar lighters claimed to give eight hundred lights for one penny, and hat pads for glossing silk hats.

Unfortunately problems arose because of the different rates of expansion of enamel and iron. The resistance wires used also contained iron, which rusted when exposed to the atmosphere and withstood neither prolonged high temperatures nor frequent switching. Consequently premature failures occurred and little progress was made with space heaters until 1896, when a practical *lamp radiator* was designed by H. J. Dowsing.

Another solution was offered thirteen years later by a Bastian *radiant heater* in which the resistance wires were protected from rusting by quartz tubes. But the problem of element failures had already been solved in the United States in 1906 by L. Marsh. He patented a heating element made from nickel and chrome which did not rust and was long lasting even at high temperatures.

This was the breakthrough the manufacturers had been waiting for and a flood of exciting new heating appliances appeared. In 1910 Dr S. Z. de Ferranti advocated the use of *parabolic* reflector

4

fires. This was followed by a revolutionary development in 1912 when C. R. Belling wound nichrome heating coils on strips of fireclay.

A safety requirement for such heaters was that the first heater bar should not be switched unless a visual indicator light was fitted. Other requirements were that portable appliances should not be used in bathrooms, exposed metal required earthing, conductors should be insulated or totally enclosed and capable of carrying the maximum current without overheating. Also flexible cords had to be anchored with clamps, surface temperatures controlled and provision made for expansion. The provision of fireguards became compulsory in 1952.

Although an imitation coal fire was made in 1913 by the Falkirk Iron Company, a new dimension was added to electric heating in 1920 by H. H. Berry, who invented the flicker effect.

In addition to the luminous radiant heaters so far described, heat was also provided by convection, that is by heating and circulating the air. Several attempts were made to improve convectors by fitting velocity tubes or designing them like Valor oil stoves. Fans were also fitted but were noisy and it was not until 1953 that *fan-assisted heaters* became popular following the production of a silent tangential fan heater in Germany.

Like the early Crompton non-luminous radiators, convectors gave no visual indication of heat but both Dowsing and the GEC overcame the problem with *radio-convectors*. Later radiant heating elements were added to convectors to make them more acceptable.

By the 1930s electricity was being used for heating an amazing variety of heating appliances. Typical examples were bowl fires, utility heaters (for both heating and

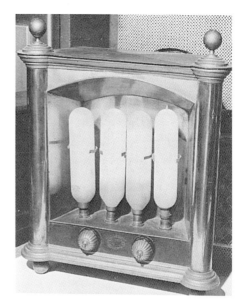

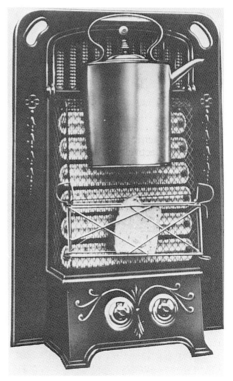

TOP: *In this Dowsing radiator cosy-looking 'sausage' lamps with carbon filaments were mounted in front of reflectors to give immediate warmth. The heat output was usually limited to four 250 watt lamps. About 1912.*

RIGHT: *In this Belling fire six 500 watt elements heated the fireclay strips to near incandescence and improved the heating performance. Trivets, toasting attachments and pegs — to hang flat-sided kettles on — were supplied as extras. About 1912.*

5

The Premier bowl and parabolic reflector fires on the left reflect the infra-red rays in straight lines and fill the space with spreading beams of heat. On the right is a small fire in a ceramic surround. About 1930.

cooking), blankets and bedwarmers. One bedwarmer could be used as a 'belly warmer' for the relief of stomach ache; another was a combined foot, bed and food warmer and night light. Less typical appliances were sealing-wax heaters, carpet heaters, heated footstools, Rota-heaters, around which fan blades driven by hot air revolved, and hexagonal 'family' fires, around which people sat.

The decorative styles of the Art Nouveau and Art Deco periods influenced design, and some early heaters were shaped like sunflowers. Later, chromium-plated fires in the form of sailing yachts made a brief appearance. Other heaters were made to resemble Grecian urns, lyres and Egyptian pyramids. Another unusual heater was the storage heater in which heat was stored in blocks of iron or soapstone, usually during the night, for use the next day. Although developed in 1904, it was not widely used until after the Second World War when the icy winter of 1947 caused supply problems. Within the next ten years improved heaters using bricks and other storage materials were developed, and in 1962 the electricity supply industry introduced its Unit Plan domestic heating campaign for which cheap off-peak tariffs were offered.

REFRIGERATION

Electricity can be made to drive machines such as fans, cleaners, washers and refrigerators by passing it through the coil windings of an electric motor. This creates powerful forces of electro-magnetic attraction and repulsion, which cause an armature or rotor to rotate at high speed.

Refrigerators are appliances for removing heat and are of two kinds, *compression* and *absorption*. In the former electricity supplies mechanical energy and in the latter heat, and both work on the principle that heat always flows from a warmer object to a colder one.

The upper part of an insulated refrigerator cabinet contains a freezer compartment around which a refrigerant is circulated which *boils*, that is changes from a liquid to vapour, when low temperature heat from the food flows into it. In a compressor-type refrigerator this vapour is drawn off by a compressor pump driven by an electric motor. This raises its temperature above room level, forces the heat-laden vapours into a condenser, which dissipates its heat to the atmosphere, and causes the refrigerant to liquidise and start the cooling cycle again.

Most refrigerators nowadays are of the compressor types which use R134A, which is HFC KLEA or ISO butane, a hydrocarbon. The first refrigerators used ammonia, which boils at minus 28F (minus 33C), as the cooling medium. Other refrigerants used included brine, sulphur dioxide and methyl chloride.

Ammonia gas in aqueous solution, with the addition of hydrogen, was used in absorption-type refrigerators, which had an absorber in the cooling circuit to separate the ammonia hydrogen gas mix-

6

ture. There were no moving parts and a small electric heater caused the refrigerant to boil up through a tube to the top of the cabinet, and the rest of the cooling cycle was then carried out by gravity and in silence.

The first compressor-type refrigerator for domestic use, the Domelre, was marketed in the USA in 1913. This was followed by a Kelvinator refrigerator the next year, and another wooden cabinet water-cooled machine was made in Detroit in 1918. This was the Guardian, a name which was later changed to Frigidaire, and in 1923 Frigidaire started to

RIGHT: *A realistic flickering effect was produced in this Siemens Excel fire by slotted discs fixed above red lamps and made to revolve, by means of the rising hot air, below panels of imitation coal made of coloured glass. About 1930.*

BELOW: *The Falco fires on the left and right have heating elements of resistance ribbons on mica formers; about 1912. The Tricity Sunray heater (centre) has a radiator lamp behind copper reflectors, which provides a cosy glow, and a radiant element at the top; about 1920.*

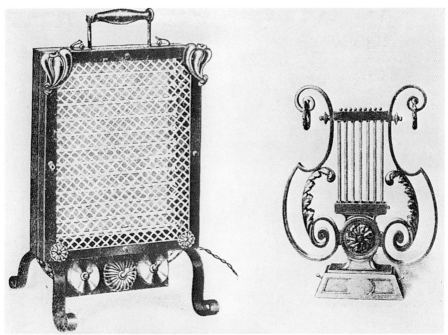

ABOVE: *(Left) A Bastian Quartzalite fire in which the elements are protected by quartz tubes; about 1910. (Right) A Lyre fire in which the strings are replaced by seven Bastian heating elements; about 1927.*

LEFT: *An Alsthom soapstone storage heater; about 1924. Bottom left and right and top centre are storage-type bedwarmers. The other warmers resemble hot-water bottles, and that at bottom centre can also be used as a belly warmer; about 1920-30.*

ABOVE: *This early Kelvinator domestic refrigerator had a bulky wooden cabinet with a compression-type refrigerating unit mounted on top; about 1914.*

RIGHT: *This BTH refrigerator had a 'beehive' cooling unit mounted on the top; about 1932. Later refrigerators had the compressors housed in the bottom of the cabinet, and legs disappeared.*

export smaller and cheaper refrigerators to Britain. They sold for £60.

Four years later Electrolux started making absorption refrigerators in Britain which had wooden cabinets and sold for £48. These had to be permanently connected to the cold water supply, but by 1932 a small 1 cubic foot (28 litre) Electrolux model in a metal cabinet was marketed. Although less efficient than the compressor type this required no running water and was silent and cheap, selling for £19 15s.

Initially refrigerators were slow sellers but the Food Preservative Act of 1927 limited the use of preservatives in perishable foods and gave an impetus to refrigerator sales. In the unusually hot summer of 1934 food storage in the home became a problem, and suddenly people became interested in refrigerators. By

1939, two hundred thousand British homes had one but they were unlike anything seen today. Firms such as the GEC and BTH entered the cooling business and produced their popular 'beehive' refrigerators. By the time pioneering firms like Frigidaire and Kelvinator were making refrigerators in Britain, smaller and more silent compressors were being developed, legs began to disappear and storage space was enlarged.

In the 1930s performance was improved when thermostats were fitted. These automatically maintained interior temperatures at around 45F (7C) except in the freezer compartment, where it varied between 0 and 18F (−18 and −8C). The method of control was either by bi-metal strips of brass and steel, which bent with variations in temperature and flipped the switches on and off, or by

9

gas bulbs in which the expansion and contraction of gases was used to operate bellows-type switches.

Most of the early refrigerators were insulated with cork, but later glass wool and expanded plastics were used instead.

In the post-war period the demand for refrigerators increased and Electrolux introduced a small one for building into planned kitchens. Another hot summer in 1959 boosted sales and further refinements included table tops, coloured cabinets and push-button or automatic defrosting. Wooden cabinets were also revived for dining room use, and in the 1960s Prestcold marketed a wall-hung refrigerator.

A large Carron double-doored cooker with the inner door made of glass; about 1900. The control switches and fuses were mounted on the wall and, as they often flashed and sparked, servants were warned not to douse them with water.

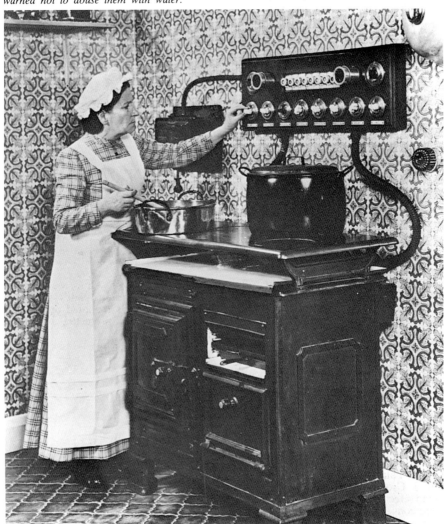

The large amounts of air space required for gas combustion were unnecessary with electricity, and ovens were made smaller and raised on legs like the Carron cooker (left); about 1922. (Right) An early Creda cooker; about 1910.

COOKING AND WATER HEATING

COOKING

Coal-fired kitcheners and gas and oil stoves obtained their heat by combustion, a method of releasing energy by burning fuels and combining them chemically with oxygen to produce heat. The most notable technological advance in cooking stove development was the replacement of chemical methods of heat production by electrical ones.

In an electric cooker electricity is changed into heat without combustion. At the turn of a switch it flows through conductors to heaters made of resistance wires. These resist its passage, get hot in the process and heat up the oven, grill and boiling plates.

In Britain electric ovens made by Crompton and Company were first demonstrated at an electrical exhibition at Crystal Palace in 1891. Other firms followed Crompton's example and marketed electric cookers, many of which were converted cast iron gas stoves, but others were made of sheet metal. Designs varied but usually included an inner oven and outer case, some with insulation in between. Others like a 1913 Tricity relied upon highly polished sheet metal casings to prevent heat loss. Above were spaces for the grill and boiling plates, the latter being radiant coils mounted on fireclay supports, usually protected by metal grids.

Electric cooking was a new concept and many early troubles arose, including rusting of heating elements. Fat and moisture also dripped on oven heaters, oven temperatures were difficult to control, and when solid hot plates with enclosed elements were introduced they tended to overheat and distort. These problems were eventually overcome and refinements such as splash plates, separate grills, warming cupboards, oven lights, oven thermometers, sliding latch ventilators and even glass oven doors became available.

Main switches were left on the walls, but the cooker switches, for which three

11

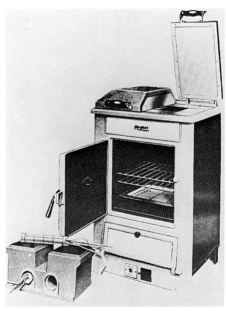

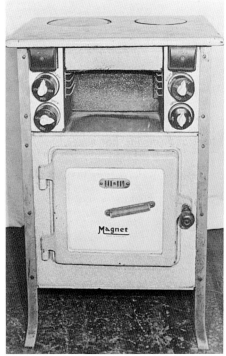

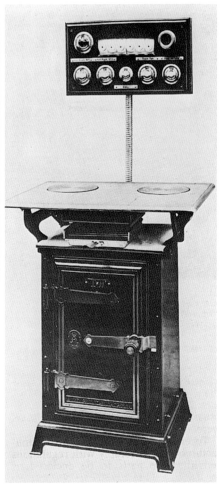

ABOVE: *A two-plate Falco cooker; about 1914. Early electric cookers were often converted gas stoves, and it was thought that if they resembled the familiar gas ones the servants would not be afraid to use them.*

TOP LEFT: *A Magnet heat storage cooker in which a cast iron block was continuously heated by two 250 watt elements with a 500 watt oven boost, via a change-over switch; about 1932.*

LEFT: *A Magnet vitreous enamelled cooker with large rotary three-heat switches, oven thermometer and sliding latch ventilator; about 1925.*

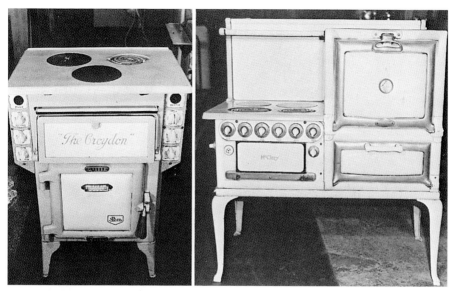

LEFT: *A Revo Superspeed cooker; about 1932. This was one of the first to have a radiant boiling ring energised at 10 volts from a step-down transformer. With 200 amperes flowing through it, the strip element glowed red hot.*

RIGHT: *A handsome McLary split-level cooker, with white enamelled door panels in nickelled frames, which eliminated stooping when attending the oven; about 1930. Although popular with housewives, it took up a lot of kitchen space.*

heat types were used to give better heat control, were mounted on the fronts of the cookers. Porcelain enamel, mostly mottled black and white, became the usual finish until the 1930s, when colours were introduced.

To ensure safety in operation, manufacturers had to comply with regulations requiring live parts to be enclosed or insulated, exposed metal to be earthed, and control units, fuses and main switches to be installed for the purpose of disconnection and protection.

From time to time manufacturers experimented with new types of cookers. In 1908, for instance, Le Radiant cooker was made with *radiator lamps* mounted inside a nickel-plated oven. Also two American cookers were being publicised in Britain in the 1920s, one with an electric oven and gas boiling rings. The other, a cast iron coal range, had a secondary electric oven and two boiling plates built into it. A more revolutionary cooker by the Falkirk Iron Company in 1925 induced heat directly into the food

from a primary alternating current coil. Although induction heating was an advanced concept it failed to influence cooker development at that time. A dual purpose cooker by Archibald Low and Sons the same year was fitted with water tanks below the hob to absorb residual heat and provide hot water.

In 1934 the Prestcold Company combined cooking with refrigeration by putting the oven above the cooking table and the refrigerator below it. Another unorthodox cooker was the Magnet heat storage cooker.

Designers gave full reign to their own ideas and there was little uniformity in the size and layout of the cookers being made by competing manufacturers. Moreover, some firms had to make thirty or more different models to satisfy the hire scheme requirements of electricity supply authorities. Greater measures of standardisation therefore became necessary. These were not easy to achieve but nine of the leading cooker manufacturers pooled their experience and, in 1930, a

(Left) Stokes table cooker; about 1920. (Centre front) Boiling plate with open coil elements; about 1914. (Right front) Bastian hot plate with elements in quartz tubes; about 1910. (Right back) Premier saucepan; about 1910. (Centre back) Jackson table cooker; about 1938.

standard specification was agreed. Among the improvements introduced were interchangeable boiling plates and removable oven interiors.

Fortunately standardisation did not halt progress and split-level cookers were made, some with 'colonial' type drop-down oven doors. Cookers with kitchen heaters also appeared and fast low-voltage radiant boiling rings, such as the Revo Superspeed, were developed. These had coiled metal strip elements coated with special enamel to prevent them from being short-circuited by the cooking pans. Additionally, lighter and faster variants of the solid boiling plates were produced, with names like Cook-quick and Speediron; bi-metal thermostats gave protection against overheating and multi-heat switches provided more flexible heat control.

The great advance in speedier heating came in the 1930s with the introduction of American-type standard voltage radiant rings, which, unlike the solid boiling plates, did not require the use of flat-bottomed utensils. Consisting of resistance coils embedded in magnesium oxide and enclosed in chromium iron sheaths, they were controlled by energy regulators. These provided infinitely variable heat control, the operating mechanism being bi-metal strips which expanded when heated and switched the rings on and off according to the control knob setting. In the late 1930s the early open coil heaters were revived in an improved form on some cookers, and cabinet cookers without legs began to appear.

By this time cooking performance was greatly improved, but one further refinement was needed, a good oven regulator. As long ago as the 1890s Crompton's engineers had invented an automatic oven controller, and in 1914 the GEC was making mercury thermostats to give four-step oven control. Yet it was not until 1931 that a reliable automatic temperature controller became available for electric cookers which matched the flexibility of the gas regulo. The first to be manufactured in Britain was the Credastat as fitted to Creda cookers.

Domestic cooker production virtually ceased in 1940, and when it resumed in full after the war cookers were more or

14

ABOVE: *(From left to right) A Samovar coffee percolator; Cona coffee maker; Hawkins Tecal bedside tea maker and night light; an Autopress coffee percolator; and a Universal tea infuser. About 1920-30.*

BELOW: *(Front) A simple toaster with cast iron enamelled base; about 1914. (Left and right) Two side-opening toasters; about 1930. (Centre back) A Universal pop-out automatic toaster with clockwork timer which produces seven graduations of toast; about 1938.*

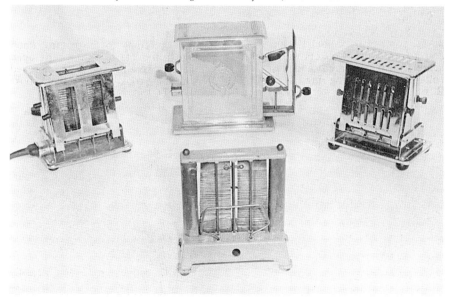

ABOVE: *Kettles for kitchens were usually functional, but those for dining rooms displayed greater craftsmanship and were more elegant. All metal kettles were highly polished or plated to reduce heat loss. About 1920.*

BELOW: *Some of the earliest electric water heaters were portable copper urns. These were particularly useful for providing hot water for large-scale tea and coffee making. About 1890.*

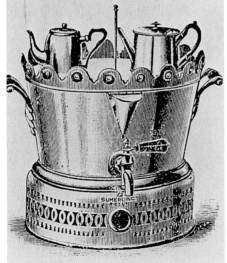

less the same except that new materials were used. Most of the cast iron was replaced by pressed steel, and the English Electric Company even made an aluminium Ritemp cooker. To meet the rising expectations of post-war housewives refinements such as auto-timers, multi-circuit radiant rings and simmerstats were added. Control switches were also raised to more convenient positions.

Although Tricity built-in cookers were installed in a London housing estate in 1932, it was not until the 1970s that separate ovens and hobs became fashionable.

Over the years many small table cookers, such as the Stokes table cooker, were made. The firms of Bulpitt and Hawkins both added steam cookers to a wide range of small culinary appliances which included boiling plates, saucepans, egg whisks, food and drink mixers, chafing dishes, warming plates, waffle plates, frying pans and even electrode egg boilers. Coffee percolators, tea infusers, tea cosies and milk warmers proliferated and a bedside tea maker was introduced in 1920 by L. G. Hawkins.

An important early appliance was the simple toaster, a British invention first made by Crompton and Company in

This rather cumbersome portable cleaner by the British Vacuum Cleaner Company was called 'a maid of all work'; about 1914.

1893. Later side-opening types were developed, some of which reversed the toast when opened. Then from the USA in 1926 came the pop-up model. This sometimes gave a spectacular performance by ejecting toast high in the air, often in flames! The end-opening automatic pop-out toaster of around the same period was less sensational.

The most popular supplementary appliance for use with cookers was the electric kettle, which was first exhibited in 1893. The early ones were slow boilers with the heating elements embedded in the bases, where they could not be renewed. By 1911 the heaters were being clamped underneath the kettles and could be replaced if faulty. 'Insertion' heaters for converting utensils for electrical operation were also being made.

The traditional shape of electric kettles changed little over the years, although some innovative manufacturers occasionally altered the design. In the 1920s, for example, a combined kettle and platewarmer, the Hotplate, was marketed, as also were a wall-mounted kettle and a kettle combined with an automatic tea-making machine. Later, in the 1930s, a dual-purpose kettle and egg steamer was made, and Bulpitt produced a combined kettle and saucepan, with separate heaters for boiling and simmering, and a whistling kettle.

What eventually established the electric kettle as the fastest and most economical water boiler was the enclosure of the heating element in a metal tube so that it could be totally immersed in the water. This method was patented by A. L. Large in 1922.

A problem with kettles was that if they were allowed to boil dry the heating elements burnt out, and as early as 1904 fusible cut-outs were used as safety devices to disconnect the supply when overheating occurred. Many other methods were later used including float switches and spring-loaded resettable self-ejecting connectors.

Although Metro-Vic Supplies produced a self-regulating kettle in 1929, it was not until 1955, when Russell Hobbs marketed a vapour-controlled one, that automatic kettles became popular. In this advanced kettle a jet of steam caused a bi-metal strip to expand and switch off the supply when the water boiled. Another bi-metal safety switch prevented damage to the kettle if it was switched on when dry.

Most early electric kettles were made of copper but some were made of tin, aluminium, glass and porcelain. Close relatives of the kettle were porcelain boiling jugs. Some of these had the heaters wound around the outside; others had the live resistance coils immersed in the water. As a necessary safety precaution the lids could not be opened while the electricity was connected.

WATER HEATING

Among the earliest appliances for heating water by electricity in the 1890s were portable copper urns with heating elements clamped underneath. Geysers were also used in which water, flowing through a small container, was instantly heated. To prevent the electricity being switched on before the water started to flow, taps were usually linked to the switches. The snag was that to heat water instantaneously high loadings were required which created havoc with the electricity supply, causing lights to flicker and dim.

Other methods of heating water were therefore explored, and in the early part of the twentieth century Therol iron block thermal storage water heaters with loadings of only 500 watts were made but were not popular. Much more acceptable were the electric heaters introduced in the 1920s for heating water, especially in existing hot tanks. One of the earliest was the Santon electric tank belt for wrapping around cylindrical tanks. A more efficient method was to insert an immersion heater into the storage tank. Although flat disc and rectangular shapes were made, most heaters were rod types which were of two kinds, *immersion heaters* and *circulators*.

During the same period two types of thermostatically controlled self-contained storage water heaters were made: *free outlet*, in which the cold water entering the bottom caused hot water to overflow down a pipe without a tap; and *pressure* types with internal or external cisterns supplying tap outlets. Both were lagged

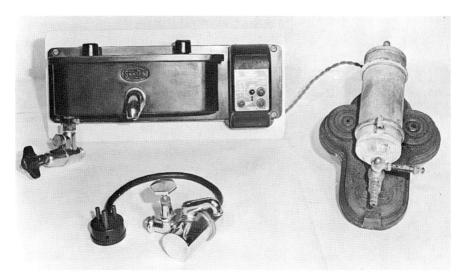

ABOVE: *The Santon geyser has a bare wire heater within an insulated container; about 1935.* *(Below) A Hot Tap heater with resistance plate heater; about 1940. (Right) A geyser on a cast iron base with resistance wires wound round copper water tubes; about 1910.*

against heat loss, usually with granulated cork.

Among the new ideas developed before the Second World War was the Highlow automatic ball valve cistern tank. In this the outlet pipe was attached to a float which rose and fell with the water level. Consequently all the hot water could be drawn off without being cooled by the inlet of cold water.

An unusual domestic water heater was the Valtair Aquatherm *electrode heater* for heating milk and water and humidifying the air. It was heated by two carbon electrodes in the bottom of a container consisting of an inner and an outer vessel made of porcelain. When switched on, electricity flowed through the liquid contents, which, being a poor conductor, resisted its passage and became heated.

After the Second World War the need arose for a self-contained water heating system for use in new housing projects. For this purpose the under the draining board or UDB cistern-type heater was developed.

CLEANING AND WASHING

CLEANING

The vacuum cleaner was a British invention by H. C. Booth. While watching a demonstration of a commercial cleaner, which unsuccessfully attempted to blow dust into a box-like container, he conceived the idea of sucking dirt up instead of blowing it about. Having proved to his satisfaction that this would work, he made a prototype suction pump — the first ever vacuum cleaner. After patenting this in 1901 he formed the Vacuum Cleaner Company Limited the following year and at first specialised in commercial cleaning. In 1926 the com-

pany's name was changed to Goblin (BVC) Limited.

However, it was in the United States in 1908 that the lightweight portable domestic vacuum cleaner originated — almost by accident. J. M. Spangler, who lived in Ohio, suffered from asthma, which was aggravated by the dusty nature of his work as a janitor. Hearing of Booth's invention, he constructed a portable cleaning machine with an electrically driven extractor fan to suck up the dirt disturbed by a revolving brush.

W. H. Hoover saw Spangler's prototype and was quick to recognise its sales

RIGHT: *Spangler used a broomstick for the handle and a pillow case for the dust bag when making the prototype suction cleaner for which patent number 889823, dated 2nd June 1908, was granted.*

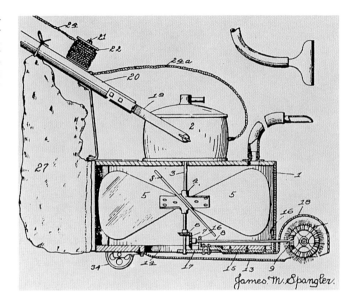

BELOW: *The BTH Newmode cleaner, on the left, can be used for cleaning curtains and such like by attaching a hose to the handle; about 1920. On the right is one of Goblin's most successful cleaners, the Wizard; about 1930.*

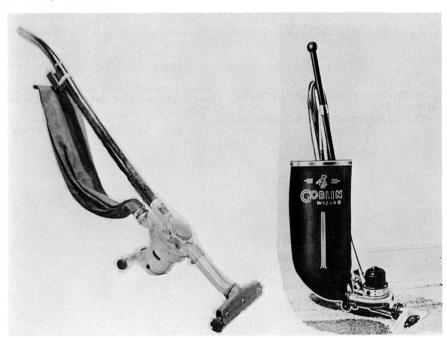

potential. He therefore acquired the marketing and manufacturing rights and set up a company to make and sell 'suction carpet sweepers'. From about 1912 Hoover's cleaners had been appearing in Britain, and nine years later Booth developed a lightweight upright 'bag and stick' model to compete with them.

The market for domestic cleaners was enormous and many electrical firms, such as the GEC, Reyrolle, Ediswan and many others, were quick to cash in on such a lucrative business. A setback occurred during the 1930s slump, but hire purchase schemes and door to door selling were introduced to stimulate sales.

As well as the bag and stick cleaners, canister types, first patented in 1910 by P. A. Fisker of the Danish firm of Fisker and Neilson, came on the market. Early examples were the Tellus, Electrolux and Cannon cleaners.

WASHING

In 1908 John Fisher, an American engineer, made the first electric washing machine. He fitted an electric motor to a hand-operated washer and drove the mechanism via a belt. Unfortunately such motors tended to get soaked with water.

Six years later this problem was overcome by fitting bottom drive *dollies* or *agitators* and tucking the motors away beneath the wooden tubs. The next stage was to fit a wringer above the tub, gear-driven by a vertical shaft from the motor below.

(Left) A Reyrolle Eureka bag and stick cleaner, and (right) a Tellus suction cleaner; about 1926.

The introduction of metal tanks and power-driven wringers made it necessary for them to be earthed, for cable connections and switches to be protected from water, and for quick-release safety mechanisms to be fitted to wringers to prevent fingers being trapped.

Most of the washers stood on legs and had tanks in which agitators rubbed the clothes, and above which a wringer was mounted. There were, however, variants. In a Napier-Kimber washer of the 1920s the clothes were cleaned by the tank being shaken up and down.

A Savage combined washer and spin dryer, which originated in the USA, was also marketed in Britain by the Berry Electrical Company, and the GEC made a *drum-type* washer called the Thistle.

This had a U-shaped trough in which a hollow wooden cylinder revolved to and fro.

In 1923 a washer from Germany used coal to heat the water and electricity to spin a *perforated drum* backwards and forwards. This was followed two years later by a British washer by T. Balmforth which used gas for heating and electricity for power. In the 1930s, too, some unusual washers appeared, like the Hera, a small box-shaped tank with a centrifugal pump attached. The clothes were washed by pumping hot soap suds through them. The most novel washing machine was undoubtedly the Magic vacuum cup washer of 1935 by MacGregor and McCullam Ltd. Instead of an

21

agitator it had an ingenious arrangement of three nickel-plated washing cups which produced the action of human hands.

Despite these innovative ideas the conventional agitator-type washer retained its popularity and emptying pumps were fitted, more attractive and colourful finishes appeared and water heaters were installed. After the war round tanks gave way to squared-off cabinets without legs, and with compartments for the storage of wringers and hoses. In 1947 a Thor combined clothes washer and dishwasher appeared, and in 1953 a Vibrosonic sound wave washing device was advertised which worked on alternating current at 28 volts. In this a diaphragm vibrated at frequencies of up to five thousand a second, and shook the dirt out of the clothes.

LEFT: *The first power-operated washing machines were converted hand-operated washers. They were driven by belts from electric motors, usually fixed beneath the wooden tubs. About 1908.*

BELOW: *A Beatty washing machine with copper tank alongside a Servis machine with tripod legs; about 1930.*

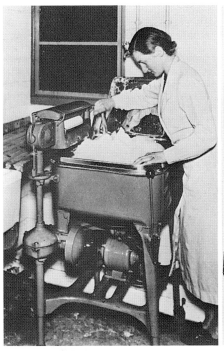

ABOVE LEFT: *A Hotpoint Maytag gyrafoam washer with cast aluminium tank; about 1928. Knife cleaners, mincers, sausage machines and ice-cream makers could also be operated from washers with powered wringers.*

TOP RIGHT: *This unusual Napier-Kimber washing machine had no internal agitator, and the entire tank was externally oscillated up and down by an electric motor; about 1920.*

RIGHT: *A simple wash boiler in which the clothes were washed by the movement of the hot water, plus a lot of elbow grease; about 1924.*

For those unable to afford washing machines, simple wash boilers were developed in the 1920s. Some were fitted with wringers and later ones, in 1947, were converted by Hoover into small washers by fitting impellors into the side of the tanks. Within the next nine years wringers were made obsolete by the revival of spin dryers. As their drums revolved at high speed, the supply was automatically disconnected and a brake applied when the lids were lifted.

Two things began to affect the design of washing machines in the post-war period; man-made fibres and detergents. Some fibres could be harmed by very hot

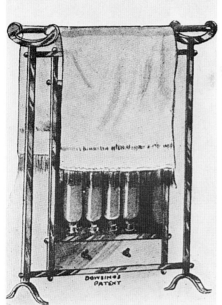
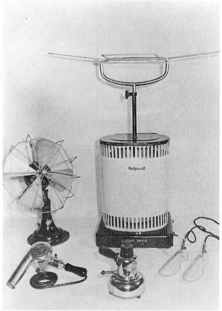

LEFT: *A Dowsing clothes dryer and towel rail in which the heat is provided by four radiator lamps; about 1910.*
RIGHT: *(Centre) A Hotpoint clothes dryer with a heater at the bottom and a folding rack above. (Left) A Revo oscillating fan. (Below) Two hair dryers and a pair of Ronning footwear dryers. About 1920-30.*

water and with detergents less water and heat were required. Smaller machines were, therefore, made and in 1957 Hoover installed a spin dryer in the same cabinet as the washing machine and produced its first twin-tub washer. This was the forerunner of today's automatic machines. Another kind of washer was the dishwasher, a domestic version of which became available as far back as 1922.

DRYING

The housewife's need for clothes dryers and airers was met by portable, wall-mounted and cabinet-type models. The cabinets had electric heaters at the bottom, some of which were fan-assisted, and racks above. In 1956 spin dryers were revived and two years later domestic tumbler dryers became available. Other drying appliances were towel rails, footwear dryers and motor-driven hair dryers. A different kind of hair dryer was an electrically heated comb by Simplex.

Ventilating fans were also used for drying clothes.

IRONING

To get clothes smooth and shiny they had to be ironed, and the first electric iron appeared in France in 1880. It was heated by an electric arc consisting of two carbon electrodes between which a brilliant arc of electricity hissed and spluttered. A safer arrangement was to wind a resistance ribbon on a mica former and clamp it on top of the sole plate. The first iron of this type was cordless and had to be placed on a stand and plugged in to heat it up. A more convenient arrangement was to connect the irons directly to the electricity supply by flexible cords so that the heat could be continuously applied while ironing. By 1891 both Crompton's and the GEC were selling improved irons of this sort.

At first most irons were for use on 100 volt supplies, but Universal irons were available by 1912, especially for travelling

24

A selection of irons. The travelling iron (top right) has a plated carrying case which can be filled with water and heated by the iron for shaving. The large laundry iron (top centre) weighs over 15 pounds (6.8 kg). About 1900-30.

irons, which had multi-pin connectors for either 100 or 200 volt operation.

An attempt at heat regulation was made in 1930 when a dial thermometer, with temperature settings for different materials, was fitted to an electric iron. The same year a Safeguard automatic heat control connector was introduced, and by 1936 a thermostat giving a choice of five temperature settings became avail-

Early domestic appliances, about 1905-40. In the front is a tailor's iron weighing 20 pounds (9.1 kg); about 1905. Behind this is a small Cannon suction cleaner with spoked wheels; about 1920. To the right of this is an early Hoover cleaner; about 1912.

able. Although an Eldec steaming iron was made in the USA in 1926, another twenty-seven years elapsed before the Hoover steam-or-dry iron was marketed. in Britain.

Flat-bed ironers and rotary ironers were made for domestic use but were never popular because of their bulk and weight. A lightweight trouser presser was, however, more widely used. Among the odd-looking irons were egg-'shaped ones for milliners, half egg-shaped glossing irons for polishing shirt fronts, hat irons and corset irons.

HEALTH AND BEAUTY

During the 1870s, when electricity was increasingly used by the medical profession for curative treatments, it was also being exploited by non-medical entrepreneurs as a panacea for almost every ailment. Not only were 'temples of health' opened by so-called 'consultant medical electricians', but a variety of do-it-yourself electrical and magnetic 'apparatuses' for health and beauty were advertised. These ranged from electric helmets to grand celestial beds!

For the Victorian girl who desired a beautiful body a Harness electropathic corset at a cost of a guinea or so was alleged to invigorate the wearer and provide her with a sylph-like figure. The flat-chested youth who longed to become a virile specimen of manhood was catered for as well. Dr Moffat's electropathic belt was claimed to restore him to health and vigour and bring a glow of health to his cheeks.

Appliances for health and beauty were

Rotosurge Number 567 and Readson high frequency apparatus. Similar devices were sold with charts listing sixty ailments which could be treated by means of glass electrodes. About 1930.

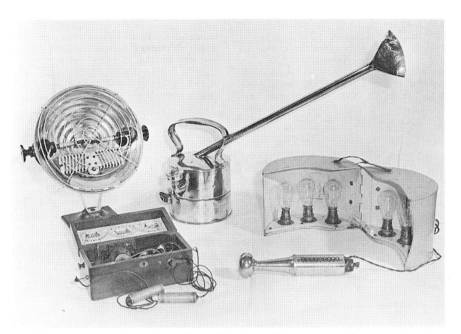

(Top left) A Gamage's Pifco sunlamp; about 1930. (Bottom left) A magneto-electric machine; about 1912. (Centre) A Rosamon bronchitis kettle; about 1910. (Top right) A lumbago belt or heat bath; about 1912. (Bottom right) A vibrator; about 1920.

legion. Dr Scott's hairbrush was alleged to cure nervous headaches, prevent falling hair and even the softening of the brain. Electric combs, teeth cleaners, therapeutic pendants, electropathic socks and vibrators all had their place in the hocus-pocus of health and beauty treatments.

Among the many other appliances were high frequency machines for the treatment of anything from barber's itch to writer's cramp. An unusual machine was the Rotosurge Number 567, which looked like a portable gramophone. A wide range of glass electrodes was used with such machines for applying treatments to different parts of the body. The application of high voltages to these electrodes at very high frequencies caused blue, violet or pink glow discharges to take place and streams of sparks to be emitted at the points of contact with the patient's body.

The application of heat has long been regarded as beneficial for rheumatic complaints, and infra-red and ultra-violet ray sun lamps were prolific, as also were heat massagers, heat baths and lumbago belts. Other appliances used extensively before the days of air conditioning were bronchitis kettles. These have long spouts and are now much sought after by collectors.

For the treatment of nervous diseases hand-operated magneto-electric machines were once popular. These make interesting display pieces and are still popular with children, who like the tingling effect of the electric shocks they produce.

Old advertisements and catalogues show that an astonishing variety of electrical aids to health and beauty were at one time available, some powered by dry batteries. The latter included Overbecks' Life Rejuvinators, Electrollers and Electrovivers.

Although often exploited for pseudo-medical purposes by over-zealous salesmen, electricity was used extensively by genuine medical practitioners with excellent results.

A period advertisement for the Medical Battery Company Limited advertising electropathic belts; about 1900.

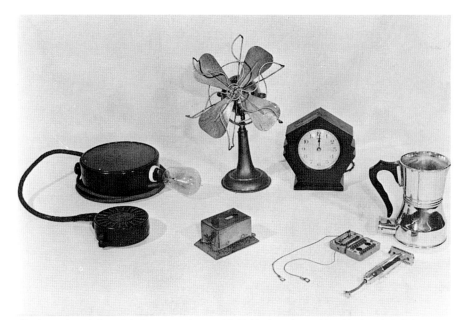

(Clockwise from left) A BQ Ozoniser; about 1930. Table fan; about 1925. Clock with Bakelite case; about 1930. Shaving jug; about 1926. Electric razor and honing device; about 1933. Spill lighter; about 1910.

MISCELLANEOUS APPLIANCES

In the early part of the twentieth century portable electric motors with gearing for driving over fifty different domestic appliances had been developed. Self-contained power appliances were made later and the advent of miniature electric motors had, by the 1930s, increased their range to include such things as Hydro-Pulsator teeth cleaners, clocks and electric razors. Small table fans also became something of a status symbol in affluent homes, and dual-purpose types with table lamps or fruit bowls attached were advertised as 'admirable wedding presents'. Some fans oscillated or had blades at the back and front, and in 1934 a Nastrovent fan was marketed with fabric blades suitable for nursery use. Table fountains made an appearance as also did Sterizaire air-conditioners, which circulated, humidified and disinfected the air. Similarly, ozone generators which produced breezes and ridded the home of flies were also made.

For the home brewer a Gee-Gee distil-ler, complete with two glass flasks for receiving the alcoholic liquor, became available.

The first electric shaver was designed in 1928 by Jacob Schick, an American, and worked rather like hair clippers. A small electric razor from Germany was being advertised in Britain in 1933, and the Philips shaver with circular cutting head arrived four years later.

Among the more bizarre appliances were devices for electrocuting rats, mice and cockroaches. But of all the electrical appliances which have been marketed the most extraordinary contraption was surely the Waker-Upper of the 1930s. This awoke a person in the morning with an audible alarm and then stripped the bed clothes off to dissuade him or her from going to sleep again.

CONCLUSION

In its early days electricity was a luxury for the few. It was such a novelty that society ladies sometimes printed the word

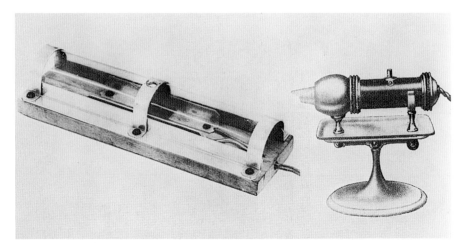

(Left) Pieces of cheese were dropped through the hole in the top of the electric mouse trap. To reach it the mice had to tread on live contacts. About 1926. (Right) A Magnet pipe lighter; about 1921.

'Electricity' on their invitation cards so that people could come and inspect their new glow lamps. Tea parties were also held at which guests could sit in the drawing room and watch Booth's men vacuum cleaning the carpets and draperies.

Today electricity is a necessity and the novelty of its use has long since worn off. Early appliances which now look crude and old-fashioned alongside their modern counterparts are, nonetheless, nostalgic reminders of our past with a character and charm of their own. This has inspired collectors to seek them out and preserve them for posterity.

(Left and centre) Novelty table fans combined with fruit bowls and reading lamps. (Right) A chafing dish for heating or cooking food at the table. About 1910.

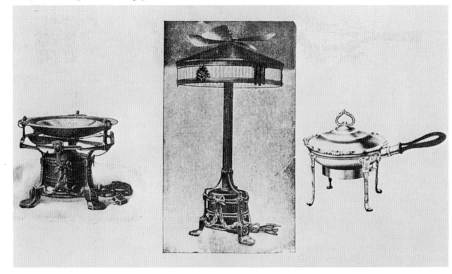

A period advertisement showing an early cooker with a built-in water heater and a selection of other domestic appliances; about 1908.

FURTHER READING

Byers, Anthony. *Centenary of Service*. The Electricity Council, 1981.
The Goblin Story. Goblin (BVC) Ltd, 1969.
Gordon, Bob. Article on vacuum cleaners in *Antique Collector*, March 1982.
Hann, David de. *Antique Household Gadgets and Appliances*. Blandford Press, 1977.
Matthews, R. Borlase. *Electricity for Everybody*. The Electrical Press, 1912.
Watford Magazines. Watford UDC Electricity Department, 1908.
Electrical Reviews. Electrical Review Ltd, 1900 40.

PLACES TO VISIT

Readers are advised to check the opening times before travelling.

Amberley Museum and Heritage Centre, Amberley, Arundel, West Sussex BN18 9LT.
  Telephone: 01798 831370. Website: www.amberleymueum.co.uk
The Museum of Science and Industry in Manchester, Liverpool Road, Castlefield, Manchester
  M3 4FP. Telephone: 0161 832 2244. Website: www.mosi.org.uk
Science Museum, Exhibition Road, South Kensington, London SW7 2DD.
  Telephone: 0870 870 4868 / 020 7942 4000. Website: www.sciencemuseum.org.uk
The Museum of Electricity, The Old Power Station, Bargates, Christchurch, Dorset
  BH23 1QE. Telephone: 01202 480467. Website: www.scottish-southern.co.uk/museum

A cleaning demonstration by the BVC Company at a London society tea party; about 1902.